Overthrowing EVIL ALTARS

Pastor Uzor Ndekwu

Overthrowing EVIL ALTARS

Pastor Uzor Ndekwu

MEMOIRS
Cirencester

United Kingdom:

Uzor Ndekwu Ministries (Jesus Sanctuary)
25/27 Ruby Street
Old Kent Road
London SE15 1LR
United Kingdom
Tel: +44 207 277 5664; +44 7961 276 187
Email: info@jesussanctuaryministries.org
Website: www.jesussanctuaryministries.org

Nigeria:

Uzor Ndekwu Ministries (Jesus Sanctuary)
41 Otigba Crescent
GRA
Onitsha
Anambra State
Nigeria
Te: +234 803 395 0197; +234 803 405 2113

Published by:

Uzor Ndekwu Ministries (Jesus Sanctuary)

Bible quotations are from the King James Version of the Holy Bible.

Printed by

Memoirs Publishers
England

ISBN 978-1-909874-91-6

CONTENTS

	Page
ACKNOWLEDGEMENTS	(i)
INTRODUCTION	(iii)
CHAPTER 1 - WHAT IS AN ALTAR?	1
CHAPTER 2 - KINDS OF ALTARS	18
CHAPTER 3 - PURPOSES OF EVIL ALTARS	81
CHAPTER 4 - MANIFESTATIONS OR SYMPTOMS OF ATTACKS FROM EVIL ALTARS	94
CHAPTER 5 - PRAYER POINTS	123
CHAPTER 6 - HOW TO RAISE AN ALTAR	135

ACKNOWLEDGEMENTS

I wish to express my profound gratitude to God Almighty for the revelation of this book. I thank God for the grace He gave me and others who worked with me to see this book to completion.

I especially want to thank Brother Andrew Chukwueweniwe who worked tirelessly with me in the writing of this book. I also want to acknowledge the typing up of the manuscript by Sister Amara Chukwueweniwe. I cannot fail to also express my gratitude to Brother Emeka Ndekwu, Sister Josephine Ife and Brother Collins Ife who also spent a lot of time with me in the writing of this book.

My thanks also go to the editor, Ms Elyssa Campbell-Barr, who did a fast and effective job in the editing of this book – her suggestions were very much appreciated.

Finally, I am also indebted to my wife and family, as well as many of my Christian brethren who, in one way or another, contributed to the success of this book with their ideas, additions and support. God will bless you all in Jesus' name, Amen.

Uzor Ndekwu

INTRODUCTION

My affection for elderly people began when I was a young lad. I enjoyed assisting my elders whenever the need arose, and always derived great joy from offering a helping hand to the older generation.

As an adult, I was close to my maternal grandparents, who both lived to well over a hundred years of age. Because he was the oldest man in the village, my grandfather held court in his compound, as the chief custodian of the village shrine or altar.

The day-to-day activities of the village shrine or altar are undertaken by shrine priests. They are like the ministers of the shrine, carrying out the duties demanded by those who wish to engage the services of the shrine in dispute resolution.

The shrine priests report to the village council

of elders whenever a matter is contentious, especially if it relates to their functions and services. My grandfather's compound, being the 'traditional official court', was always busy with local activities or meetings to do with the village shrine.

In one of my weekend visits to my town, I decided to see my grandfather as usual. As I approached his compound, I noticed an unusual number of people both within and outside. I could tell from their faces that they were agitated. I was surprised that I could barely recognise any of them and their accent was obviously different. I immediately knew they were not from my village.

As I remained in my car, pondering the situation, I beckoned to one of the people outside the gate. When I asked what was going on, he told me the following story.

A young man from the neighbouring village had confessed that he was the cause of a strange death in his business partner's family. He had used the village shrine to settle a fraudulent business transaction between him and his friend, whom he felt had cheated him.

This confession, and the fact that there had indeed been some unusual deaths in the family, had prompted the parents and relatives of these estranged business partners to come to my grandfather's compound. They wanted to ascertain the facts of the matter and – if the confession was true – decide how to appease the gods of the shrine and put a stop to the strange deaths.

The matter was further complicated because some of the shrine priests had not been consulted before the activities and services of the shrine had been deployed. One of the shrine priests had acted alone, meaning the traditional rules of engagement with the shrine had not been followed.

It was the need to address this situation and take steps to appease the gods to prevent further deaths in both families – as well as the larger implications of not following the traditional process – that the elders in my grandfather's compound were discussing, which prevented me seeing my grandparents that day.

About six weeks later I visited my grandfather again, keen to know how the matter had been resolved and what steps had been taken. He told me that, after the traditional cleansing and appeasement of the shrine, the matter was settled amicably. The shrine priest who had acted without recourse to traditional procedures was reprimanded and fined some goats, which were used as a sacrifice of atonement to appease the gods of the shrine.

Continuing, my grandfather recounted other incidents that had almost wiped out families who had abused the traditional procedures of dealing with the shrine. He cautioned of the dangers in the use of shrines to settle family, business, marital and other disputes, because the consequences of such acts normally result in strange deaths.

I asked why the village elders should allow or encourage use of the shrine's services in these modern times. I also queried why the village should not have a traditional council to settle matters without recourse to the shrine gods.

My grandfather told me that the shrine or altar had been their forefathers' method of handling contentious issues that had financial or material implications. He added that matters brought before, or involving, the shrine tend to be resolved easily because people know the consequences of lying when under an oath involving the shrine.

For him, the shrine had played an extrajudicial role in the peace, orderliness and stability the community had enjoyed over the years. He told me that, because of the effectiveness of this village shrine, neighbouring towns and communities were using its services in settling some serious matters. The shrine, therefore, was an integral part of the community in dispute resolution.

Nevertheless, he continued, one thing he had observed over the years was that those who had employed the services of the shrine in dispute resolution never experienced progress. He began to list the names of families who had used the shrine to settle disputes, and explained that they had all suffered setbacks in their lives. He told me plainly that, no matter what, issues should never be taken to traditional shrines or altars for settlement.

At this point, I was a bit confused by my grandfather's counsel. I asked him to clarify why he allowed court to be held in his compound for issues or matters related to the shrine. He told me that, as the oldest person in the village, tradition bestowed on him such responsibility. His view was that his role was largely ceremonial; that the shrine priests were actually the key players in the affairs of the shrine.

Finally, I asked him why the shrine always worked against those who served it or used its services. He responded that the rules of the shrine are usually strict and that people must, either deliberately or not, be flouting the rules governing the shrine's communities or societies.

For example, my grandfather explained, one of the rules of the shrine is that, once you engage the gods of the shrine to battle another person, none of your kindred or relations may interact with the person the gods are afflicting, under any circumstances. The day any blood relations of the person who engaged the shrine gods relate to or interact with the person being afflicted, the same afflictions, diseases and calamities brought by the shrine gods are visited upon the relatives of the person who initially contracted the shrine's services.

I said that was unfair on the part of the shrine gods; that given the extended family system we have, some may not know about the activities of other members of the nuclear or extended family. He replied that was why he had cautioned earlier that it is never good to use the services of the shrine in any shape or form.

As I drove home, I began to reflect on our discussions about shrines. I concluded that, on the balance of probabilities, evil or satanic shrines or altars are two-edged swords that are destructive both to their users and their victims. The bottom line is that nothing good will ever come from the domain of Satan. No matter the role of judgemental altars of Satan in dispute resolution, the spiritual consequences of covenanting with such demonic altars outweigh their perceived role in dispute resolution in communities or societies.

There are numerous ways to get to the truth in disputed matters or issues without recourse to satanic altars. This could be one of the reasons God told Moses that satanic shrines or altars must be destroyed as they journeyed in their land of promise:

> *"But ye shall destroy their altars, break their images, and cut down their groves: For thou shalt worship no other god: for the LORD, whose name is Jealous, is a jealous God:"* (Exodus 34:13-14).

By implication, therefore, in order for you to actualise the plan and purpose of God for your life, relationships, businesses, families, communities, children and other personal endeavours, you must have the spiritual understanding that any demonic altars that you find, or which are erected against you, must be overthrown.

The first question is how would you define or recognise satanic altars? Secondly, how did these evil altars originate? Thirdly, how many kinds of altars exist in our world? Fourthly, what are the symptoms or physical manifestations of those under satanic altar attacks? How do you deal with them, and what does the Bible recommend on how to go about it?

The answers to these probing questions are in the subsequent pages and chapters of this book.

CHAPTER 1

WHAT IS AN ALTAR?

Simply put, an altar is a place or platform dedicated for sacrifice, service, atonement, offerings, petitions and supplications to a superior being; that is, either to God, the creator of Heaven and Earth, or to other gods (idols) that exist, or may have existed, in other times and places. From a broader perspective, an altar is a meeting place among spirits, and between the physical and spirit worlds. In one word, an altar is a 'gateway' in the realm of the invisible *(Genesis 28:12-13)*.

It is also good to differentiate between thrones, altars and temples. Thrones are seats of judgement in the realm of the spirit *(Genesis 41:39-41)*, while altars are places of intervention that are used by man *(Genesis 28:12-22)*.

Temples are dynamic in nature as they are highly individualised – every human being is a temple that either carries the spirit of God or the spirit of Satan *(1 Corinthians 6:19)*.

According to the Scriptures, the first altar raised by man to God was the altar built by Abel and Cain, where they offered their first fruits unto God *(Genesis 4:3-8)*. After the flood, Noah raised an altar of thanksgiving and supplication, which activated a new covenant and promise from God. The Scripture says:

> *"And Noah builded an altar unto the LORD; and took of every clean beast, and of every clean fowl, and offered burnt offerings on the altar. And the LORD smelled a sweet savour; and the LORD said in his heart, I will not again curse the ground any more for man's sake; for the imagination of man's heart is evil from his youth; neither will I again smite any more every thing living, as I have done.*

While the earth remaineth, seedtime and harvest, and cold and heat, and summer and winter, and day and night shall not cease." (Genesis 8:20-22).

As a result of this sacrifice by Noah, God responded favourably by establishing a covenant with him:

"And God said, This is the token of the covenant which I make between me and you and every living creature that is with you, for perpetual generations:" *(Genesis 9:12).*

Altars are raised for different reasons and purposes. When God appeared to Abram, he built an altar to commemorate His presence *(Genesis 12:7-8)*. In Exodus, Moses raised an altar for God *(Exodus 17:12)*. When David wanted to stop the afflictions that came upon his people, he built an altar *(2 Samuel 24:25)*. As Joshua journeyed towards the Promised Land, an altar was raised to God *(Joshua 8:30)*. The mighty Gideon also raised an altar unto God *(Judges 6:24)*. These are just a few of many examples.

On balance, these altars by these servants of God were raised basically as a memorial of thanksgiving, appreciation or anticipatory goodwill, to draw the attention of God to pressing needs or issues. Altars are, therefore, physical manifestations of sacrifices, and sacrifices are like the soul and spirit of an altar. What makes an altar powerful is not its material content, but the quality of the sacrifice offered on that altar. It is the quality of the sacrifice that defines, determines and confirms the spiritual connections between the raised altar and the heavenly realms.

What differentiated Abel's and Cain's altars, and caused the eventual acceptance of Abel's offering by God, was not the altar raised, but the quality of the sacrifice. The sacrifice offered to God upon any altar is a mirror of the quality of the heart towards God, our creator. The depth of gratitude towards God is normally reflected in the size and quality of the sacrifice we make upon God's altar.

One of the things that made King David a man after God's own heart was the quality of his sacrifices to God. King David said he would never give God anything that did not cost him something. King Solomon, David's son, was also noted for his generous sacrifices to God.

What made God swear upon Abraham's blessing is the quality of the sacrifice he attempted to offer Him when he obeyed God's instruction to sacrifice his son, Isaac, upon the altar at Mount Moriah. What moved God to take an oath over Abraham's blessings was the special nature of, and circumstances surrounding, Isaac's birth. Abraham had waited for Isaac for nearly twenty years. For Abraham to attempt to sacrifice Isaac without any doubt or fear showed his love towards God. He was totally committed to God, and God reciprocated by making him a channel of blessings from generation to generation. Abraham, by this act, challenged God at the altar of sacrifice. He became a spiritual icon in the act of sacrifice.

What made Mount Moriah an altar of God – and ensures it remains to this day a popular pilgrimage site for Christians, Muslims, Jews and other religious faiths – is the quality of uncommon obedience demonstrated by Abraham there. Before the Cross at Calvary, Mount Moriah was one of the most revered altars, because it was at that spot that Abraham spiritually offered his son, Isaac, in obedience to God's command. Although God later provided Abraham with a ram that was sacrificed in place of Isaac, the provision of that spiritually spotless animal by God made the altar of Mount Moriah a spiritual epicentre. The foundation of any altar is, therefore, rooted in the quality of the sacrifice offered upon it.

When Jesus Christ willingly offered himself and

was sacrificed on the Cross of Calvary, the Cross became the highest and most symbolic altar because of the circumstances and nature of the sacrifice. Jesus' sacrifice of Himself voluntarily is obviously superior to animal sacrifices. Beside its superiority, Jesus' sacrifice is the most powerful from substitutionary and redemptive perspectives.

All the sacrifices, beginning from the Garden of Eden, through Abraham's ram sacrifice at Mount Moriah, to Moses' institutionalisation of the sacrificial Old Covenant, cannot be compared to Jesus' sacrificial death at Calvary *(Matthew 26:28; Hebrews 9:14-15)*. Jesus' death completely put away sin *(Hebrews 9:26; 1 John 3:5)*. The Old Covenant sacrificial imperatives only covered sin temporarily and necessitated repetition of the sacrifices whenever the need arose. In terms of redemption, it was not a wholesome package.

However, Jesus' sacrifice became the mother of

7

all sacrifices because it signalled a completed and permanent act, undertaken voluntarily *(Hebrews 10:10-17)*. The Scripture says by this obedience:

> *"...he obtained a more excellent ministry, by how much also he is the mediator of a better covenant, which was established upon better promises."* *(Hebrews 8:6).*

The Cross on which Jesus was sacrificed became a powerful symbolic altar in the physical and spiritual realms because of the quality and nature of the sacrifice.

The foundation of the altar in the New Testament, which is anchored in Jesus' sacrificial death, is far superior to altars in the Old Testament. The Old Testament altars were anchored in the unwilling, unjustified and unspotless animal sacrificial systems, which were inadequate in dealing with the needs of the spiritual man. The animal blood foundation that birthed the Old Testament can only meet the carnal needs of man. As noted in the Scriptures:

> *"For if the blood of bulls and of goats, and the ashes of an heifer sprinkling the unclean, sanctifieth to the purifying of the flesh."* (Hebrews 9:13).

The blood of Jesus, which is the foundation of the New Covenant Cross, purifies not only the flesh, but has obtained eternal redemption for mankind. The sacrificial death of Jesus Christ made His tabernacle, symbolised by the Cross, spiritually effective. Through His death, Jesus became the mediator of the New Testament, surpassing the promises and covenants of the Old Testament. By implication, Jesus' tabernacle became superior to that of Moses for two main reasons:

Firstly, in the Old Testament, Moses' tabernacle and the Ark of Covenant, the most sacred item in the tabernacle, were built and made by man – the hand of flesh. In the New Testament, the tabernacle of Jesus Christ, which the Church represents, was not made by the hand of man, but by God. As the Scripture says:

> *"But Christ being come an high priest of good things to come, by a greater and more perfect tabernacle, not made with hands, that is to say, not of this building;"* *(Hebrews 9:11).*

The regenerated body of true believers in Christ has the ability and capacity to become a dwelling place of the Holy Spirit. The body of man became a 'mobile tabernacle' for the Spirit of God, which was not possible in the old dispensation. That is why Apostle Paul encouraged believers to present willingly their bodies as living sacrifices, holy and acceptable unto God. This, he says, is our "reasonable service" *(Romans 12:1).*

Secondly, on the issue of blood, both tabernacles are qualitatively, comprehensively and redemptively different. The blood of calves, rams, goats and other living creatures formed the foundational sacrificial system of the Old Testament. The blood of these creatures had been defiled, touched by evil owners and not separated from sinners. The sacrificial blood of the Old Testament only served to sanctify the flesh. It was ineffective in redeeming, reconciling and delivering mankind from the powers of darkness, as noted by Apostle Paul in Hebrews 9:13.

The blood foundation of the Old Testament, which was the cornerstone of Moses' tabernacle, was fundamentally limited. The need for a new testament was inevitable. It came through the sacrificial death of Jesus Christ on the Cross of Calvary. The foundation of the New Testament covenant, and the tabernacle therefrom, was based upon the blood of Jesus Christ.

The blood of the New Covenant was both comprehensive and redemptive. It responded to the demands of the flesh and the spirit. It met the needs of man and God. The blood of Jesus addressed the obvious shortcomings in the Old Testament. It became possible to put away sin, and not just to cover over sin, as provided by the Old Covenant animal sacrifices. Furthermore, the opportunity for total forgiveness, reconciliation with God, and to live in holiness and righteousness became possible. Jesus, by His sacrificial death, provided the blood that destroyed the power and works of the devil. Mankind, therefore, became redeemable.

Thirdly, the tabernacle of Moses, based on the Old Testament, did not witness the death of the testator (Moses). Through the process of animal sacrifice and the sprinkling of the blood on the altar and the people, he constituted the tabernacle of the Old Testament *(Exodus 24:6-8).*

However, in the New Testament, Jesus'

tabernacle witnessed the death of the testator. He offered Himself as a priest and the sacrificial lamb on the Cross, as ransom for the sin of all. This made His sacrifice the mother of all sacrifices of the things in heaven, earth and beneath. This was a complete and perfect sacrifice. It put paid to all and any other sacrifices – animals, fowls of the air and other living creatures.

The New Testament has acquired an upgraded spiritual legitimacy and power that the Old Testament lacked, which made it wholly inadequate to deal with the comprehensive expectations of mankind. The free-willed and obedient sacrifice of Jesus Christ is far better than the involuntary animal sacrifices in the Old Testament. In the Scriptures, Apostle Paul said that Jesus' sacrifice was the final statement in the realm of sacrifice *(Hebrews 9:15-26)*. Because it was comprehensive and perfect, with no need ever to be repeated, it is indeed the mother of all sacrifices.

Be that as it may, it must be noted that the Old Testament was not replaced or supplanted by the New Testament. The Old Testament Scriptures are not outdated. However, the Old Covenant, based on Mosaic law and sacrifices, was upgraded. The sacrificial death of Jesus Christ, which introduced the New Testament, brought grace and mercy that offered an alternative to Mosaic law and punishment.

Another vital difference between the Covenants (Old and New) is that the varied and yearly sacrifices in the realm of atonement were replaced with the final sacrificial death of Jesus Christ on the Cross of Calvary. The Old Testament can never be obsolete. Some Biblical scholars' opinion that the New Testament replaced the Old Testament is an error in assumption and conclusion.

Jesus Christ's tabernacle is fundamentally the same as Moses' tabernacle. That is why Jesus Christ said that He did not come to destroy the law:

"Think not that I am come to destroy the law, or the prophets: I am not come to destroy, but to fulfil. For verily I say unto you, Till heaven and earth pass, one jot or one title shall in no wise pass from the law, till all be fulfilled."
(Matthew 5:17-18).

In any case, the law is indestructible, because it is the word of God, which is God Himself:

"In the beginning was the Word, and the Word was with God, and the Word was God... And the Word was made flesh, and dwelt among us, (and we beheld his glory, the glory as of the only begotten of the Father,) full of grace and truth."
(John 1:1,14).

Nonetheless, as I mentioned in the previous pages, His sacrificial death on the Cross of Calvary essentially brought in grace and mercy. By implication, therefore, the Old Testament covenant promises and provisions are still effective in the matters of the flesh and in the domain of the spirits.

The blood of goats, bulls and humans can equally be used in spiritual issues between the visible and the invisible realms, and can be very effectual, either negatively or positively. From the positive perspective, in some cultures and traditions, goats, rams and bulls are still being used in altars as sacrifices to appease the gods in some matters, as I mentioned in the introduction to this book referring to my experiences in the village.

On the other hand, the blood of living creatures (human beings, animals, fowls of the air) is being used in satanic altars for wicked activities against perceived victims. In the Scriptures, Balaam and Balak raised seven altars after satanic ritualistic sacrifices, with seven oxen and seven rams in order to curse the children of God:

"And Balaam said unto Balak, Build me here seven altars, and prepare me here seven oxen and seven rams. And Balak did as Balaam had spoken; and Balak and Balaam offered on every altar a bullock and a ram." (Numbers 23:1-2).

Just as in the Biblical time, in most contemporary traditional societies the blood of these living creatures is just as effective in a limited way. The sacrificial death of Jesus Christ, which ushered in the New Testament, did not cancel the Old Testament blood covenants, but it is superior in all realms (heavenly, earthly and water) to the blood of living creatures. This is because the blood of Jesus is the blood of the spirit, and the spirit world is more powerful than the physical world. Therefore, animal sacrifices, and the blood therefrom, can only work in satanic altars, which are in the domain and authority of man.

CHAPTER 2

KINDS OF ALTARS

Our discussion of evil altars must start from the source or genesis of such altars. How did the evil altars come to be? Who started them? Are there any Biblical accounts of such altars? How do you identify an evil altar, and for what purpose?

When we talk about altars, we generally talk about sacrifice and atonement. Sacrifice has to do with the heart. The heart has to do with intention, and intent determines the sort of altar to be raised. From the Biblical account, men of God who raised altars did so as a thanksgiving for an encounter with God and a place that manifested His glory. The hearts and intentions of these men of God were good, and that reflected on the sort of altars raised unto God.

Altars are, therefore, a fruition of thanksgiving

and supplication towards the goodness and manifestation of God in one's life. They are like a mirror of man's love towards God.

When Abel and Cain raised altars of thanksgiving, God accepted Abel's sacrifice and rejected that of Cain. Cain's attitude towards God was reflected in the sort of sacrifice he offered unto God. Sacrifice is a reflection of the premium or value we place on our relationship with God.

The Tower of Babel (tower for short) is another altar that God not only rejected, but also obstructed by mixing up the languages of the builders. In my estimation, the tower is a classic case of an evil altar. Indeed, the tower was built purposely as an affront to the sovereignty of God. The builders were trying to reach heaven from their earthly base, which is an obvious rivalry with God.

Moreover, they were trying to make a name for

themselves, which betrayed the Adamic nature in man. It revealed man's efforts to be independent of God and to act according to his own free will.

The builders' intention was to unify all mankind under one authority, and create a universal sovereignty that would be in a position to contend with God:

"And the whole earth was of one language, and of one speech. And it came to pass, as they journeyed from the east, that they found a plain in the land of Shinar; and they dwelt there. And they said one to another, Go to, let us make brick, and burn them thoroughly. And they had brick for stone, and slime had they for morter. And they said, Go to, let us build us a city and a tower, whose top may reach unto heaven; and let us make us a name, lest we be scattered abroad upon the face of the whole earth. And

*the L*ORD *came down to see the city and the tower, which the children of men builded. And the L*ORD *said, Behold, the people is one, and they have all one language; and this they begin to do: and now nothing will be restrained from them, which they have imagined to do. Go to, let us go down, and there confound their language, that they may not understand one another's speech. So the L*ORD *scattered them abroad from thence upon the face of all the earth: and they left off to build the city. Therefore is the name of it called Babel; because the L*ORD *did there confound the language of all the earth: and from thence did the L*ORD *scatter them abroad upon the face of all the earth.*" *(Genesis 11:1-9).*

It is clear that the purpose of the tower, which technically is an altar, was not worthy, but was for selfish reasons. God had no other option than to confuse the builders' tongues, which arrested man's ambition of building a rival altar from the earth to reach heaven.

However, there are some ongoing repercussions of the scattering of the builders of the Tower of Babel upon the face of the earth by God. It gave rise to diverse societies of people with different tongues. This, by implication, gave rise to the foundation of diverse gods and deities. Although man was not able to build a tower that reached the sky (which would have been a challenge to God), people nonetheless raised diverse kinds of altars upon the face of the earth. Each altar reflects difference in geography, culture and language.

There are diverse communities all over the world, and each has its own gods and deities. The gods in Asian nations are different from the gods in African nations, which may be different from gods in other parts of the world. Even within the same country, there are gods that represent, or are a reflection of, different cultural backgrounds.

For example, in Nigeria, as in other African communities, different regions have different manifestations of satanic altars, reflecting their different cultures, environments and tongues. In India, it is reported that there are over 330 million gods!

The satanic or demonic altars raised in any given area are a reflection of the kinds of gods being worshipped. Coastal regions deal more with marine altars, which harbour marine spirits, while the hinterlands deal with altars that harbour demonic spirits. This accounts for the necessity of spiritual mapping before embarking on any spiritual battle in any given geographical location. The demonic forces that operate in the UK are different from the ones that operate in the USA, China, Japan, Togo, and so on.

The beginning of satanic altars can be traced to the dispersion of the builders of the Tower of Babel, because the hearts of the people involved were evil and wicked towards God. They were not God-oriented, but were instead selfish in their ambition to reach heaven, which was the original quest of Satan – to ascend unto the Throne of God. That led to him being overthrown and thrown out of heaven with some fallen angels.

According to Biblical story, Nimrod, one of the grandsons of Noah, was the 'chief initiator' of the building of the city and the tower, and his heart was set against God. God knew that the heart that gave birth to the tower (which was a form of altar) was evil and meant to challenge God. The issue here for God, I think, was not the building of the tower to reach heaven – it was the heart and the intent of the builders, for a wicked heart can only give birth to a wicked altar, and altars can be instruments of challenge, defence and protection in the realm of the spirit.

The toppling of the tower became imperative. God decided to mitigate the evil imaginations of man, but by not destroying man again because of His covenant undertakings with Noah in Genesis 8:21: *"And the LORD smelled a sweet savour; and the LORD said in his heart, I will not again curse the ground any more for man's sake; for the imagination of man's heart is evil from his youth; neither will I again smite any more every thing living, as I have done."* Instead, the tongues of man were divided in order to frustrate a unified front against God. There are some lessons to be learnt here:

1. POWER OF IMAGINATION

In the Scriptures, the Lord said:

> *"... Behold, the people is one, and they have all one language; and this they begin to do: and now nothing will be restrained from them, which they have imagined to do."* (Genesis 11:6).

Whatever you imagine or purpose to do, you can actualise. For instance, the world came into being by God's imagination. Western civilisation and all its technologies come from imagination, and this has widened the gap between the West and the rest of the world. The power of imagination, which the West exploited, has given these nations a massive advantage over the rest of the world. Although the natural resources of the world (gold, silver, oil, diamonds, etc.) are in Third-World countries, the West has exploited the rest of the world through this very same power, and it is this that Western nations are using to control the world.

2. DIVERSE LANGUAGES

According to the Scriptures, God confused the tongues of the people:

> *"Go to, let us go down, and there confound their language, that they may not understand one another's speech."* (Genesis 11:7).

Creating diverse languages through the act of

dividing their tongues meant the world can never be unified. The colonial masters used this Biblical principle to dominate and rule other nations of the world. For example, the British Empire, wherever they ruled, would bring people of different languages and cultures together as one nation, in Africa, Asia and elsewhere. Apart from the economic benefits, this had a more profound function: to perpetually rule them. In doing so, they gave them a common language – the English language.

In Nigeria, there are three major tribes (Hausa, Ibo and Yoruba), and over 250 ethnic groups. That is why, after over fifty years of independence, the country cannot be one – because of the different languages. In the Indian subcontinent, there are Indians, Pakistanis, Bangladeshis and Sri Lankans, and they could never be united together. The Kashmir issue between India and Pakistan was created by the colonial masters and persists today. However, this policy of bringing different nationals together did not work in the American colonies. The colonies united and fought them.

Be that as it may, some wicked people build altars to destroy the destinies of their victims. Such altars are erected for the trafficking of demonic spirits in order to influence or activate negative outcomes in the lives of their victims. In *Numbers 23:1*, Balaam hired Balak to raise seven satanic altars against the children of God to place a curse on them. No wonder Moses commanded the people that they must destroy satanic altars – *"break their images and cut down their groves"* – if they want to succeed in the land of their promise *(Exodus 34:13)*. Later Elijah, in his own time, turned the hearts of the people back to God. Before he destroyed the evil priests who encountered him, he first and foremost destroyed and burnt their altars *(1 Kings 18:37-40)*.

Altars are, therefore, powerful instruments in the hands of the wicked, which explains why countless families, relationships, businesses and communities have been hindered by the activation of satanic and demonic altars. Because of a lack of spiritual knowledge, the people perish *(Hosea 4:6)*.

The altars people raise are determined by the purpose to be achieved. In the subsequent pages you will read about different kinds of altars, and the purposes for which they have been raised.

TYPES OF ALTARS

From my counselling experiences (including confessions of 'native doctors' and former occultists that the Spirit of God arrested through the power in the name of Jesus Christ), the following typify the various types of altars that are common within our society. The environment, culture and language influence the type of altars in use in any given locality.

1. EFFIGY ALTARS

The effigy is one of the earliest instruments the evil ones use against their victims. Based on the confessions of some native doctors, whom God touched through our television programmes, we know that a sculpted image, representing an individual to be afflicted, can be made. As the effigy of the person is placed on the evil altar, all sorts of negative and destructive pronouncements are made on that image. Depending on the sort of affliction intended for the victim, needles, pins, keys, padlocks, and so on are placed on the carved effigy. The person represented by the effigy will begin to be afflicted or tormented demonically.

In some cases, an effigy altar may be placed in a shrine, evil forest or thrown to the river after the applicable sacrifices upon the effigies have been administered. The blood sprinkled or poured upon the effigies is to attract demonic spirits against whoever the image represents. For example, if the evil ones want to project rejection, dejection or depression on their victims, the blood of lizards or vultures is normally used for ritualistic incantations and enchantments.

Ailments that have defied medical prognosis are often caused by effigy affliction activities. It is impossible to list all the infirmities or afflictions that may result from these sorts of demonic manipulations of effigies. It is safe to pray against such altars from time to time, in relation to yourself and family members.

In the Scriptures, God exposed to Ezekiel what the ancients of Israel (the occultists) were doing in their secret chambers against their victims:

"...then he said unto me, son of man, hast thou seen what the ancients of the house of Israel do in the dark, every man in the chambers of his imagery...?" (Ezekiel 8:12).

The wicked abominations being performed against their victims are carried out through image affliction and manipulation.

Images are powerful tools of demonic attacks because human foundation is based on the image of God, which became corrupted when Adam and Eve sinned. Human beings took the corrupted image and likeness of God, through Adam, after the fall. According to the Scriptures:

> *"This is the book of the generations of Adam. In the day that God created man, in the likeness of God made he him; male and female created... And Adam lived an hundred and thirty years, and begat a son in his own likeness, after his image and called his name, Seth:* (Genesis 5:1-3).

As Adam was made in the image of God, he possessed a measure of God's power of imagination and imagery. However, sin corrupted the image of God in Adam, consequently corrupting Adam's power of imagination, thus making imagery manipulation possible.

2. PICTORIAL ALTARS

According to a former occultist who gave his life to Christ, a pictorial altar is one of the easiest altars to raise. The effectiveness of the evil afflictions or attack is based on the fact that the picture or photograph (an image of the victim) can be placed on a satanic table, floor or even pinned to a wall. The sacrifices and other evil rituals carried out on the victim's picture are meant to attract demonic spirits. In some instances, evil oil and candles (red, blue, black or white) are used to raise altars of fire. During the demonic spiritual exercise, demons are called, with the names of their victims being mentioned intently.

Evil or false prophets use such acts to cause marital afflictions or separation. I have shared the testimony of a loose woman who married a medical doctor after causing the man to abandon his wife and four children.

On a general note, just as people bring pictures of loved ones to men of God for prayers, some take pictures of those whom they hate, or want to deal with, to evil altars for satanic pronouncements.

Our own Ministries' crusade posters are normally prayed over before they are used in street placements or adverts. As a general rule, I also pray over my pictures or recordings of my TV broadcasts.

We have experience of handling cases of depression which may be the result of invocation and enchantment using pictures of victims.

3. SAND AND STONE ALTARS

Sand and stone altars are the simplest altars to raise. All you need do is to gather some stones or earth with the blood of the animal or fowl of the air to be used.

What determines the kind of blood to be used is the evil intent of the practitioner. If it is for a building project, the blood of a ram or goat may be used for invocation, enchantment and divination. If they want to slow down a project or business venture, the blood of the creeping creatures may be applied. If they want to cause confusion to the owner of the project, the blood of the fowl of the air may be used.

As the blood of any of these creatures becomes mingled with the stone or earth, after some satanic rituals, the stone or earth will have the ability to attract demonic forces. The names and images of the victims may possibly be placed on top of the stone too, and the victims' names mentioned for afflictions periodically (morning and evening).

Although earth and stone altars are very simple to prepare, they are the most effective. The stone or earth that has been negatively energised may be thrown into the compound or business premises of the victims, becoming a gateway for satanic activities.

In the spiritual realm, stones are one of the most effective instruments of warfare. What kills giants easily in the spiritual realm is stones. In the Scriptures, David used stones to kill Goliath:

"And it came to pass, when the Philistine arose, and came and drew nigh to meet David, that David hasted, and ran toward the army to meet the Philistine. And David put his hand in his bag, and took thence a stone, and slang it, and smote the Philistine in his

forehead, that the stone sunk into his forehead; and he fell upon his face to the earth." (1 Samuel 17:48-49).

In the New Testament, stones were used to bring judgement upon Stephen:

"And they stoned Stephen, calling upon God, and saying, Lord Jesus, receive my spirit." (Acts 7:59).

In the Islamic world, pilgrims are enjoined to stone Satan as the final ritualistic religious act.

When Jacob encountered God at Bethel, according to the Scriptures, all he did was raise stone and pour oil on top, and the altar at Bethel began to speak for him. It was at this altar that he achieved victory over his brother, Esau.

Sand and stones, in Biblical times, were the foundations of every altar. The Old Testament covenant was written on tablets of stone, which is an altar of covenant between God and man. In the New Testament, Jesus is known as the Rock of Ages. This symbolises the covenant relationship between God and man, because Jesus is the mediator between God and man.

The advantage of the stone and earth altar is that the altar can be raised in the premises of its victim.

4. MARKET ALTARS

The market altar derives its strength from the gathering of people of different characters, backgrounds and persuasions. There is always an energy present wherever people gather over time. Just as the Bible says that:

"...where two or three are gathered together in my name, there am I in the midst of them." (Matthew 18:20),

in the spiritual realm any gathering of people with the same intent or purpose can be converted negatively in order to afflict people.

A market is a place of interaction. Any place or premises designated as a market can equally become a gathering of demons. Most occultic people use the forces of the market to curse their victims negatively, and the demons in that market can be energised through satanic sacrifices.

The blood of animals or fowl of the air used can also generate or attract demons. Most of the ritualistic sacrifices done in the market are carried out at night, or in the very early hours of the morning. Depending on the circumstances or purpose, the footprints of the people who come to market, or to any gathering, can be collected through sweeping the market or premises, and demonic forces are easily activated to afflict the victims.

In most cases, market altars are used to cause mental, emotional and psychological afflictions. In most communities, each market day has its own 'guiding spirit'. That is why there are certain ceremonies that may never be carried out on a particular market day. For example, in my community, burial ceremonies are excluded on some market days, and traditionally only certain people are permitted to run the market.

If a person is cursed within a market, it takes a superior power and anointing by a man or woman of God to annul such satanic decrees. Conversely, if you want to dislodge any negative power operating within a town, the first place to uproot and overthrow altars is the market square. Every member of the community comes to the market or eats from the market, so they are, in one way or another, linked to the operating forces in the market square.

It is interesting to observe that when Jesus Christ discovered that money-changers were trying to turn a temple into a 'market', He reacted very strongly and overthrew the market setting in the temple. This is because He knew that two strange altars cannot operate within the same premises – darkness and light can never co-exist.

In our time, most churches that have used their premises for informal markets, selling, for example, books, shares, mortgages or works of art, have not only destroyed the spiritual fervency of the church, but have opened a gateway for demonic forces to operate in their church. This usually signals the end of spiritual fervency in such churches.

5. ASTRAL ALTARS

According to a former occultist who is now a minister of God, an astral altar is used by those who engage in astrology or star reading. The practitioners utilise the potential in the powers of the heavenly bodies (sun, moon, stars and other planets), to deal with their victims.

As you may be aware, everybody has a star, and you can be traced through your star. In Joseph's dream, he talked about eleven stars that made obeisance to him, signifying his brothers *(Genesis 37)*. The wise men from the East who visited Jesus Christ in Bethlehem, traced Him through His star to the very place where He was staying – the manger *(Matthew 2)*.

People's stars, therefore, can be traced, programmed or even manipulated. Deborah, the prophetess, spoke words to the heavenly bodies when she was fighting alongside Barak against Sisera and the enemies that attacked the people of God:

> *"They fought from heaven; the stars in their courses fought against Sisera."*
> *(Judges 5:20).*

Most occultic people deceive, engage with and manipulate people who are ignorant of 'astral altars', for their selfish ends. Many lives have been destroyed through such satanic manipulations and wrong interpretations of stars. In some cases, mental disorder or depression, waywardness, or outright madness, can be attributed to astral manipulations.

6. CRYSTAL BALL ALTARS

As the name suggests, a crystal ball is a ball-shaped object used mainly for divination and enchantment. Satanic agents and false men and women of God often use such altars to decode the future of their victims. In some instances, images of people can be conjured to appear on the crystal ball, and arrows of affliction can be released against the victims.

What empowers such altars are the sacrifices carried out on the object within the crystal ball altars. The blood from these sacrifices attracts demonic presence, and the secrets of the victims can be released by the demons. Because crystal ball altars have reflective capacity, victims' images can be invoked on such altars.

Most witches who are into divination effectively use the demonic presence that controls the crystal ball altars. The witch at Endor may have used such an altar to call up the familiar spirit of Prophet Samuel (1 Samuel 28).

Some false men and women of God use such altars to obtain information about people, and then use it for control and manipulation for their selfish ends. They speak as if they are hearing from God. This practice is absolutely demonic and has no place or relationship with the gifts of the Holy Spirit (1 Corinthians 12), which deal with Words of Wisdom and Words of Knowledge. Words of Knowledge is a revelation about somebody's past, while

Words of Wisdom is a revelation about somebody's future, which comes purely from the Holy Spirit. However, as with most things, Satan corrupts the gifts of God.

7. POT/BOX ALTARS

Pot or box altars are one of the most wickedly effective types of satanic altar. Images, items of clothing or even body parts of the victims are normally deposited in such altars. Usually, after some satanic sacrifices involving blood of living creatures, constant projections using the names of the victims, are made.

Some years ago, my son fell ill and we thought it was just malaria. However, despite the anti-malarial medicine given to him, his condition didn't improve, and his temperature was consistently high except for few hours of periodic relief. On the seventh day of his illness, the workers and I had just ended a night vigil in the church.

My wife left us to go inside and check on the children, where she found that my son's body had become quite hot again. She told me that at that point she was about to come and call me, when the Spirit of God ministered to her to pray against any evil pot where our son's name was being called and cooked for evil. She said that she had never heard such a thing, but considering the situation, she began to pray – this was not the time to ask questions.

After just three minutes, my son broke out in a sweat, opened his eyes, smiled at her, and fell asleep. His body temperature returned back to normal, and that was the end of the illness. Once I came in, she told me what had happened, which was when I remembered that in my place (Ubulu-Uku), the evil people use pots to project infirmities, afflictions and death against people.

Evil pots are also used as instruments of

judgement and destruction. We see this in the Scriptures:

"And the word of the LORD came unto me the second time, saying, What seest thou? And I said, I see a seething pot; and the face thereof is toward the north. Then the LORD said unto me, Out of the north an evil shall break forth upon all the inhabitants of the land." *(Jeremiah 1:13-14).*

Altars of evil pots are instruments of warfare commonly used by witches, wizards, occultic people and native doctors to cast spells, magic charms, enchantments and divinations against their targets.

In the case of my son, the altar of a pot was used to project infirmities against him. Such evil altars are why some people who fall sick never seem to get better, despite receiving medication for their ailments. These ailments usually manifest as constant fevers, headaches or body pains, where the purpose of such attacks is to eventually kill the person.

Evil pot altars are also used to manipulate people and circumstances. This is usually referred to in my community as 'remote control'. A good example commonly seen is those who eat in their dreams. Evil food is cooked and projected to the person in their sleep, using all manner of spells and evil manipulations. Once the person eats this food, they wake up feeling ill. Many have contracted incurable diseases and all manner of ailments in this way. In 2 Kings 4:39-40 we see a case of food that was deadly until the intervention of the prophet of God.

The Bible says:

"Therefore thus saith the Lord GOD; Your slain whom ye have laid in the midst of it, they are the flesh, and this

*city is the caldron: but I will bring you
forth out of the midst of it."*
(Ezekiel 11:7).

Some evil people take the names, pictures or
body parts (hair, nails, etc.) of their victim,
and place them in an evil pot, using those
items as a point of contact to monitor, afflict
and manipulate their victim. Some also bury
those pots with their victim's personal items
in order to bury their star. Consequently, the
victims never seem to progress or succeed in
their lives, no matter how hard they work.

8. MARINE ALTARS

Marine altars are usually built in rivers,
streams and oceans. These altars often
contain two main instruments of marine
adoration: the effigy of the Queen of the
Coast, and a python curled around it. Other
items in such altars must include red and
white clothes. These are the main colours that
rule in the marine world.

Most often, depending on the purpose or aim of the marine native doctors, sacrifices of living creatures are made. The blood sacrifice is to attract demons of the water.

Water spirits are among the most effective demonic powers because of the link between the waters and wicked spirits in high places. In the Scriptures, Pharaoh commanded his people to sacrifice the male children of the Israelites to the goddess of the water. Pharaoh's daughter's visits to the river were more for spiritual exercise and empowerment than recreational purposes, which gave her the opportunity to rescue Moses from the water.

Marine altars are equally specifically used for divination. The divination altars dedicated to the marine powers usually have white chalk, live pythons, white clothes and small bells. All of these items are used for divination through invocation of the marine spirits.

Some false churches take their members who have challenging problems or issues – especially those looking for the fruit of the womb – to do sacrifices to marine powers for children. However, most children from the marine gods or goddesses become wayward and turn against their parents. There are even cases where such children have been involved in killing their parents. In the Scriptures, Pharaoh's daughter took Moses out of the water as a child, and nurtured and trained him to become a prince of Egypt. Eventually, Moses was the person God used to destroy the Egyptians.

9. FOREST/TREE ALTARS

Forest altars are forests that harbour shrines – a shrine being a place of spiritual interplay. They are sacred spots in the forest where trees are dedicated as altars of worship. Sacrifices of all kinds of animals and creeping things are done in such places. The victims' items, such as clothes, pictures and body parts, are placed on such demonic forest altars, and sacrifices are activated depending on the purpose.

These altars are often found in big trees in the central places of the town, such as in the market square or by the town gates, as this is where major gods of the town abide and where different families worship. The following items are usually found there: clothes of different colours (mostly white and red), white chalk and kola nuts. These items are used to appease the gods dwelling in such places. Most victims of tree altars often find themselves dreaming about forests, and they experience ups and downs in their daily lives.

It is good to distinguish between tree and forest altars. Trees are what make up a forest; some evil-doers use a single tree as an altar, while others use an entire forest. Tree altars are usually personal, for example family altars planted in the family compound.

Forest altars have to do with the community in which that forest is located, and they link everyone from that community to that forest. That is why, spiritually speaking, someone from a particular community can go to the forest to fight another person from the very same community.

The Bible gives an example of this in 2 Samuel 18:6-8:

> *"So the people went out into the field against Israel: and the battle was in the wood of Ephraim; Where the people of Israel were slain before the servants of David, and there was there a great slaughter that day of twenty thousand men. For the battle was there scattered over the face of all the country: and the wood devoured more people that day than the sword devoured."*

A pastor friend of mine once had a revelation

about a female relative of my wife. He said that in the dream he saw this lady standing at one end of a very thick forest, and at the other end he saw a man holding a machete. The man then began zealously to cut down trees in order to make his way to the lady. However, half-way through the forest, he became discouraged, dropped his machete, and went back. The pastor then saw several men coming to do the same thing, only to also be discouraged half-way through.

After talking to this female relative, she told him that several men had come to ask her hand in marriage. They all came with zeal and a strong sense to commit, but as things appeared to be moving along well, they suddenly developed cold feet and left her. At that time she was still unmarried.

The pastor began to pray for her, when God told him that it was an aunt of hers whom she was close to who was responsible for her unmarried state. She apparently did her evil manipulation using the forest of their village.

The Bible says:

"And he shall be like a tree planted by the rivers of water, that bringeth forth his fruit in his season; his leaf also shall not wither; and whatsoever he doeth shall prosper" (Psalm 1:3),

and:

But I am like a green olive tree in the house of God: I trust in the mercy of God for ever and ever." (Psalm 52:8).

From these scriptures, it can be seen that people are often referred to as trees. For this reason, trees are usually used as family or personal altars in one's compound. The Scripture says that the Lord Jesus

"bare our sins in his own body on the tree" (1 Peter 2:24).

This is a clear indication that trees are altars where sacrifices are made.

My wife had a revelation about a young man who used to attend our church. She said that she was with other church members in the man's house in the village, where some sort of celebration was going on, when the man came to greet her. She then said to the man, "Your father died of diabetes, as did your mother, and several of your aunties and uncles. You too have diabetes, and the cause is an altar in your family."

In the revelation, the young man acknowledged that my wife was telling the truth, which was when she immediately woke up. As she was narrating the dream to me, the young man in question drove into the compound; I called to him to hear what my wife was telling me.

After repeating the dream, the man said that what she was saying was true, and his family had a tree that was an altar in the family compound. He also said that both of his parents and several of his relations had died of diabetes, which came upon them suddenly. Moreover, all of these episodes of diabetes manifested once they each had a major success in their lives. The young man went on to say that he himself now had diabetes, and he had got it immediately after he had a financial breakthrough and bought himself a very classy car.

As highlighted above, trees and forest altars cause a lot of problems in people's lives. Whereas forest altars are used as weapons of warfare against people generally, tree altars usually target a specific family for evil.

10. GATES AS ALTARS

In the realm of the spirits, the gate as an altar is the most powerful device. Among the altars that exist on planet Earth, the gate is the most effective and forceful. In short, the gate is the mother of all altars. The gate's ordinance is the most pervasive, and the keepers of gates are often the chief custodians of other altars within a particular spiritual area or hemisphere.

The importance of gates emanates from their basic function and purpose. Gates ensure access to, or entrance through, an enclosure. Likewise, movement between and within the spiritual and physical entities must be through a gateway or passageway. Therefore, the operations within and between the realms of man and God are controlled by gates and gatekeepers.

Jacob's vision in Genesis 28:17 confirms that: **"this is none other but the house of God, and this is the gate of heaven".** The Angels of God ascending and descending upon a ladder exemplify that connecting gate between the visible and invisible realms.

Gates are bases of spiritual authority and dominion in the affairs of people. Those who sit at gates are often spiritual captains of a

village, town, province or region. These
strong men and women control and
determine the decisions and matters of their
respective areas of influence *(Matthew
12:29)*. Furthermore, decisions taken at gates
are irreversible or unchangeable because
gates are the official quarters of the gods of
the land. Therefore decisions that have the
backing of the gods are either executed
against the culprits or substituted against
their accusers.

For example, in Esther 7:10, mischief returned
upon the head of Haman who planned and
executed wicked devices against Mordecai
and the Jews. Haman was hanged upon his
own gallows. God sanctioned the enemy to
be taken in their own craftiness and
meanness. According to the Psalmist:

*"he made a pit, and digged it, and is
fallen into the ditch which he has
made." (Psalm 7:15).*

Gates, therefore, are basically places of intervention, deliberation and decision-making. Gates equally function as places of information exchange, where the devils meet with their principal agents and exercise powers over the affairs of nation states, towns, villages, communities and individuals. Gates are operative offices for demons and evil spirits. Gates pertain to those who sit in the council of the kings; the nobles of their societies.

In the physical world, only a select few people control access to and through gates. Invariably they are those who consult with the spirit beings through crystal balls, Ouija board manipulation, witches and wizards. They take decisions after the application of divinations, enchantments and sorceries. That is why gates exist in most governmental set-ups, armed forces, judiciary and police departments.

The battle of the gates began in the Garden of Eden. As soon as man sinned, Adam lost power and authority over the gates. The gate as an access, entrance or passage came under the control of Satan. The key to accessing heavenly enclosures of blessings, promotion, favour, healing, miracles, and so on, was seized from Adam. As soon as Adam and Eve were driven out of the Garden of Eden (a place of abundance), and God

"drove out man and placed at the east of the garden of Eden cherubims and a flaming sword which turned every way, to keep the way of the tree of life" (Genesis 3:24),

man lost the spiritual power-base of his dominion and authority.

Satan established his own gates, commonly known as the gates of hell. The keys Adam surrendered to Satan were the symbol of earthly base and authority, Satan being the god of this world *(2 Corinthians 4:4)*.

It was the foundational authority of this key that made man to want to reach up to heaven through the earthly altar called the Tower of Babel *(Genesis 11:4-5)*. The Tower of Babel was the first demonic altar erected by man, and that was why God intervened to stop the evil project aimed at reaching heaven.

Noah's Ark was the first righteous altar built by man for the salvation of mankind. However, mankind's redemption was not possible before the Resurrection of Jesus Christ, because the gates, keys and authority of death were within the domain of Satan.

Before the Resurrection of Jesus Christ, everyone who died ended up in the place of the dead called Sheol – an environment of darkness where both the righteous and unrighteous remained, with separate compartments for the godly and ungodly. Sheol is often translated in the King James version of the Bible as 'grave' or 'pit'.

Beginning from Adam and Abel, to Abraham, Isaac, Jacob and Joseph, none accessed heaven, but were kept and locked up within the gates of Sheol and Hades. The souls of the godly were kept in Sheol, in a compartment for the righteous. The souls of the departed evil ones were kept in another compartment known as Hades, a place of perpetual darkness.

The story of Lazarus and the rich man is illuminating at this point *(Luke 16:19-31)*, with Acts 24:15 confirming the assumption of the just and the unjust being kept underneath the earth in Sheol and Hades. At this time, Satan was in charge of the gate and had the keys.

The story changed when Jesus Christ died. His

death was the game-changer. What man lost through Adam's spiritual death was restored through the physical death of Jesus Christ on the Cross of Calvary. Jesus' death destroyed the power-base of Satan, who had the power of death *(Hebrews 2:14)*. Therefore, the gates of death came under the sovereignty of Jesus Christ.

When Jesus commanded the gates to

> *"lift up your heads, o ye gates, and be lift up ye everlasting doors and the King of glory shall come in"*
> *(Psalm 24:7),*

Satan told Jesus Christ, I beg your pardon,

> *"who is this King of glory?"*
> *(Psalm 24:8),*

when I am the prince of the world and I have the keys. Jesus replied, your reign is over.

Before you is the *"LORD, strong and mighty, the LORD mighty in battle"*. From now on, I am the *"LORD of hosts, the King of Glory"* *(Psalm 24:10)*. God has given me a name that is above every name, both in the realms of the visible and invisible *(Philippians 2:9)*. Above all, I am the head of all principality, powers and thrones *(Colossians 2:10; Ephesians 1:21)*.

I strongly believe that, at this point, the gates and the head of the gates (Satan) surrendered and bowed down before Jesus Christ. Satan gave up the keys and Jesus took up the "key upon his shoulders" *(Isaiah 22:22)*. The principalities, powers, thrones and dominions of darkness were disgraced:

> *"And having spoiled principalities and powers, he made a shew of them openly, triumphing over them"*
> *(Colossians 2:15)*.

As soon as the keys were taken from Satan,

Jesus visited the compartment of Sheol and opened it up:

> *"And the graves were opened; and many bodies of the saints which slept arose. And came out of the graves after his resurrection, and went into the holy city, and appeared unto many"* (Matthew 27:52-53).

Jesus ended the captivity of the deceased when the gates and their agents were confronted. Apostle Paul summarised the end result of the confrontation:

> *"Wherefore he saith, When he ascended up on high, he led captivity captive, and gave gifts unto men. (Now that he ascended, what is it but that he also descended first into the lower parts of the earth? He that descended is the same also that ascended up far*

above all heavens, that he might fill all things.)" (Ephesians 4:8-10).

The way Jesus Christ dealt with the gates is worthy of note:

1) Jesus addressed the gates prophetically. He spoke to the gates as personalities that can hear and understand instructions. Gates are spiritual entities that are the dominion of spirits, and in the realm of the spiritual, words are uttered with authority and power, spoken with the expectation of compliance. Decrees are made to have effect.

2) When confronting gates, one must use the words of God, which are the sword of the Spirit, to penetrate and open them. When Scriptural words are used to speak to gates, the powers and rulers of darkness behind those gates are easily paralysed. Therefore demons, as well as satanic, occultic and religious barriers, hindrances, chains and ropes of darkness, become weakened and broken.

3) Every minister, pastor and church worker must possess the key of the Kingdom, which is the symbol of authority to open, shut and lock. Jesus told John

"... And have the keys of hell and death" (Revelation 1:17-18).

He told Apostle Peter

"I will give unto you the keys of the Kingdom" (Matthew 16:19),

which enabled him to release men and women in bondage, chains of Satan, false religion, covenants, shame, scandal, sickness, diseases and death. The power and authority to shut the doors and gates of hell, and equally release those in the captivity of Satan and his cohorts, is already given by Jesus Christ through His Resurrection power.

4) The gates of hell are Satan's most effective instruments against anointed men and women of God. Therefore, confronting the gates of hell is a must for every child of God who is destined to overcome his or her adversaries. From Adam to Jacob, the gates of hell confronted and defeated them. None overcame the strongholds of Satan at the gates. It is only Jesus Christ who overcame the gates and laid a foundation for the possibility of defeat of the powers and authorities of the gates of hell. That is why Jesus Christ's prayer for Apostle Peter was that the gates of hell shall not prevail against the Church *(Matthew 16:18)*. If the first prayer point of our Lord Jesus Christ centred on the gates of hell, it means that what gates represent is worth probing.

From the charge Jesus gave about the gates of hell, the gates represent all the opposing kingdoms or strongholds of evil spirits, dark angels, territorial gods, demons, principalities, powers, authorities and thrones sanctioned by Satan to hinder, paralyse, render powerless or dilute the fervency of the Church, and compromise or suppress its mission in the world.

The Church has become a shadow of its old self. It is in full retreat, spiritually speaking. The Gospel of our Lord Jesus Christ has gone full-circle in emptiness. The whole armour of God is gone and children of God can no longer stand against the wiles of the devil. Our faith is no longer based on the words of God and righteous living, but on charismatic contacts and connections with the marks of trade unionism.

The body of Christ has men and women of diverse interests, often without any passion for the souls that are perishing, under our umbrella. We can no longer stand *"against principalities, against powers, against the rulers of the darkness of this age"*. We are hopeless and helpless *"against spiritual hosts of wickedness in heavenly places".* Therefore, the children of God are not able to quench all the fiery darts of the wicked ones *(Ephesians 6:10-18).*

The work of darkness is being promoted in workplaces, churches, schools, institutions and homes. The result is that many Christians are sleeping spiritually, emotionally, financially and physically. We are yet to appreciate that spiritual warfare is a reality, and that the weapons of our warfare are not carnal but spiritual. The Scripture is absolute about this matter of spiritual warfare:

"For though we walk in the flesh, we do not war according to the flesh"
(2 Corinthians 10:3-4).

Flesh cannot pull down strongholds or gates because it is weak in the realm of the spirit. What is central and forceful in the warfare arena is prayer; specifically praying with the Word of God, which is the sword of the Spirit *(Ephesians 6:17)*. When the disciples settled for prayers, they overcame the gates of hell, of fear and intimidation. They began to proclaim the good news boldly, and miracles that announced the name of the resurrected Jesus Christ were performed at the beautiful gate *(Acts 3:1-13)*.

Spiritual warfare is not just games or an exercise in showmanship; it is a serious strategic spiritual business that demands real focus. Satan and the demons are real beings with clear goals – to promote works of darkness in our lives. They are powerful, but Jesus Christ has already made public show of them, triumphing over them *(Colossians 2:15)*. Above all, His name is the only 'spiritual currency' in all the three realms – heaven, earth and beneath *(Philippians 2:9-10)*, and Jesus is the head of all principality and power *(Colossians 2:10)*.

If we want to deal with gates and altars of darkness being used by the wicked ones to deal with, frustrate, hinder, and at times destroy, the destinies of people of God, prophetic spiritual warfare must be declared on the evil altars. God commanded Moses:

"But ye shall destroy their altars, break their images, and cut down their groves ..." (Exodus 34:13-14).

When Elijah wanted to end the humiliation of the servants of God before the Israelites, he destroyed the Baal altars and gates of wickedness before dealing with their prophets. Until you take charge of your gates, your possessions are not spiritually secured. The only way to have your possessions in peace and security is by overthrowing evil altars and gates that may be assigned or used against you and your beloved ones. In approaching this kind of spiritual warfare, we must engage the dimensions of the Word of

God, the keys, the name of Jesus, the blood of Jesus, fasting, praise and worship, and speaking in tongues. These dimensions could be combined in the underlisted prophetic prayers concerning altars and gates. Jesus confronted the gates of hell and delivered many saints held captive. As you decree and declare, you can also be victorious in Jesus' name, Amen.

Since gates are the mother of all altars, battles are won at the gate. When Rebekah was being sent out to join her new husband, one of the prayers offered for her was that her offspring would possess the gates of their enemies *(Genesis 24:6)*. For those who want control over their possessions, the ability to dictate and influence enemies' gates is vital. Gates may also be used as platforms for spiritual manipulation, control and intimidation. From the negative perspective, most wicked people deal with their victims from the gates, doors or entrances to their homes, offices, places of commercial transactions, and even places of worship.

For example, we have witnessed many sacrifices at our church entrance gates. These have ranged from sprinkling blood of fowls of the air, to different oily substances at the church entrance, and even placement of 'beggarly elements' sacrifices. They were usually carried out during the earlier hours of Sunday mornings. The detractors continued until I mocked their efforts during one of our live telecast programmes. Why the evil ones engaged in such activity is to limit or hinder the church's growth and activities. As a deliverance ministry, we must be prepared to deal with such wicked acts.

Similarly, detractors have placed demonic blood at my personal house on several occasions. At times, blood and feathers of fowls of the air are placed strategically at the gate or entrance to my house. Occasionally, we have seen dry leaves and powdery substances at the door. What the enemy is trying to do is cause sudden fear or induce affliction. Usually, I pray over such demonic things and clean up the act, and use the blood of Jesus to cleanse the spiritual mess.

Where I and my family members have overcome these violations, Mrs Onwordi (not her real name) was not so fortunate. She lost two of her sons within just eleven months. According to her, she had some domestic issues with her landlady and the matter turned nasty so that they no longer talked to each other. Every attempt she made for peace was unsuccessful. Over time, she began to notice that the landlady usually stayed in the middle of the compound gate at odd hours of the night. Mrs Onwordi remembered vividly how she once saw her naked and bathing at the gate. She alerted some neighbours but no one could confront the landlady. Two days after that encounter, Mrs Onwordi's son took ill and died suddenly. That is how she and her family were almost destroyed, until they sought help and went into serious fasting and prayers, after which they became victorious over their sworn enemy.

In my town, Ubulu-Uku in Delta State, one village that had a distinctive gate is called Udo village. Most prominent sons and daughters of this village have been in serious bondage as a result of this demonic gate erected as a village entrance.

During one of my crusades in the village, the young ones begged that we should pray at the village gate. As the prayer session progressed, I was led to uproot one of the trees. Dug up beneath were an ancient hook and pots, with all sorts of traditional artefacts. The people believed that the reason their sons and daughters were dying prematurely, or having their endeavours frustrated, may have been a result of the erected gate. The villagers were led into a series of prayers against ancient gates and altars that had been stumbling blocks to their children's advancement. We decided to begin church at the village entrance.

In concluding, gates and altars of darkness must be confronted in the spirit realm. If you want to actualise your God-given visions and dreams, you must have the mind-set that gates oppose your dreams, and since gates are strongholds, they must be battled.

Jesus Christ prayed for Apostle Peter that the gates of hell should not prevail against his future as the leader of the Christian faith (Matthew 16:18). Peter dealt with the gates solely through fasting and prayers when the disciples tarried in Jerusalem. The Power of God came upon them (Acts 2:1-4), and they were able to conquer the stronghold of fear as a gate. It is spiritually symbolic that Apostle

Peter's first miracle and demonstration of authority began at the gate – the Beautiful Gate of the Temple in Jerusalem – *(Acts 3:1-11)*, and from that day onwards Peter began to march victoriously towards his God-given vision.

Therefore, the question is: are you prepared to confront your gates as Jesus and the Apostles did? The only option is through fasting and prayers, and the prayer points at the end of this book will be useful guides as you embark on this spiritual exercise.

Altars are not restricted to those described in this chapter. The geography and language of the community, as well as the culture and environment in which people live, determine the type of altar the satanic ones use. The fundamental thing is that there are processes and rituals in any preparation or raising of altars, depending on the purpose for which the altar is being raised. Talking about purpose, the next chapter will concentrate on the purposes and ordinances of altars.

CHAPTER 3

PURPOSES OF EVIL ALTARS

In the Biblical narratives, the servants of God who built altars did so with hearts of gratitude. Sacrifices offered on those altars were for thanksgiving or supplication unto God.

On the other hand, people do erect evil altars. The hearts of the builders of such wicked altars are usually evil towards their fellow human beings. The evil altars are meant to create a sort of demonic or satanic platform for the interaction of the spirit world. Sacrifices are offered in order to activate and utilise the services of these wicked spirits against perceived enemies or adversaries. A good example of such altars in the Scriptures is the story of Balaam and Balak, where twenty one altars in total were built for satanic purposes against the Israelites *(Numbers 23:1-30).*

There are various reasons why people erect altars. In the subsequent pages we will try to summarise why such evil altars are raised in certain situations or circumstances. We can never be in a position to know, or pretend to guess, why some build wicked altars. Nonetheless, the insights of former occultists and native doctors who became converted, and the testimonies of some brethren and deliverance pastors, are useful in highlighting the purposes described below.

1. ALTARS AND COVENANTS

Generally, altars are places of sacrifice where the visible enters into agreement with the invisible. Altars are meeting places between the physical and the spiritual. An altar's function and effectiveness is defined by the covenant foundation upon which it is built. The covenant is the power or force behind every altar.

In the Scriptures, whenever Abraham built an altar for God, the covenant foundation behind those places of sacrifice was the forces of greatness, blessings, abundance and protection. This covenantal statement was activated when God spoke:

> *"...unto Abram, Get thee out of thy country, and from thy kindred, and from thy father's house, unto a land that I will show thee: And I will make of thee a great nation, and I will bless thee, and make thy name great; and thou shalt be a blessing: And I will bless them that bless thee, and curse him that curseth thee: and in thee shall all families of the earth be blessed."*
> (Genesis 12:1-3).

It was consummated the moment the Angel of God said:

> *"By myself have I sworn, saith the LORD, for because thou hast done this thing,*

and hast not withheld thy son, thine only son: That in blessing I will bless thee, and in multiplying I will multiply thy seed as the stars of the heaven, and as the sand which is upon the sea shore; and thy seed shall possess the gate of his enemies;"
(Genesis 22:16-17),

and became the bedrock of Abrahamic altars from generation to generation.

The force of this covenant speaks for those who are connected with Abraham, whether through blood or spiritual circumcision. Those who are connected to Abraham can activate the contents of this covenant whenever and wherever they are residing. This is because the covenant relationship between God and Abraham was for "seed after seed" *(Genesis 17:4-8)*. All those who are linked with Abraham can activate the contents of this covenant upon their own altars.

On the other hand, in traditional settings, the altars of our forefathers are quite important. The satanic or demonic altars that have been built to territorial spirits are covenanted. The sacrifices on crossroads, in markets, on mountainsides, in village squares, near rivers and in forests are meant to activate covenants with the local deities. The various offerings of rams, cows, fowls, eggs, blood, dogs and cooked food are tokens of such demonic covenants.

Basically, altars are used purposely for sacrifices either to God, the Creator of Heaven and Earth, or to demonic or satanic spirits for selfish ends. The families of evil altars' priests, native doctors and occultists suffer generationally.

2. ALTARS AS INSTRUMENTS OF WARFARE

While altars may be used as pillars of greatness and protection, some wicked people use altars as instruments of warfare and afflictions. These wicked or evil ones erect altars to cause purposely a particular sort of affliction or disease.

According to a former occultist, once the applicable sacrifices and rituals have been performed, the demons, or evil spirits are sent to afflict their would-be victims. No witch or wizard would attack you physically. It is done through spiritual manipulation and enchantments. The practitioners of such acts rely on the spirits. The presence of demonised items, such as sand, stones, native chalk, gift items or clothing, can be negative points of contact. The items are activators of evil and satanic aura. The evil ones can only function with the assistance or help of the evil spirits, just as believers who want to excel in life can only function effectively with the indwelling of the Holy Spirit of God and His Angels.

It is not insignificant that the devil, in the moment of temptation, queried Jesus Christ whether He was indeed the Son of God, saying:

"cast thyself down, for it is written, He shall give His Angels charge concerning thee" *(Matthew 4:6).*

Put simply, there is no neutrality in matters of the spirit. You are either a child of God or a servant of darkness. As Apostle Paul warned, we wrestle not against flesh and blood, and the instruments of our warfare are not carnal *(Ephesians 6:12; 2 Corinthians 10:4).*

3. ALTARS AS MONITORING GADGETS

Items such as mirrors, glassy or shiny objects or crystal objects are vital tools in the altars of darkness. According to a former occultist and native doctors, these items are used to monitor the progress or current status of their victims. As long as your name, image or photograph is in satanic altars, the wicked ones can invoke your appearance on these mirror-like items and you can be manipulated or influenced through such demonic processes.

In the spiritual exercise, distance is no barrier. Hundreds or even thousands of miles do not affect the potency of the spiritual operation being activated or carried out. In spiritual affairs, physical barriers or distance do not hinder the spirit's movement or effectiveness – just as in your dream state you can travel, visit and interact with people who are hundreds of miles away. The dream world that mirrors the spirit world reveals that the spirit of man is not limitable.

I have seen and handled cases where siblings who all live in different parts of the world suffer from the same afflictions or diseases. Four brothers who all had the same high blood pressure problems, and all lived in different geographical locations, died prematurely as a result of this affliction. Their only sister, who is a born-again child of God, told me that a nephew swore that he would "monitor them" unto death because of a land matter – the land being, according to her, their father's inherited property. The wicked nephew employed the services of some evil men who carried out such wicked acts.

The Scripture says that

"those who know their God shall be strong and do exploits" *(Daniel 11:32b)*.

Invariably, those who use satanic or demonic gods could hinder the destinies of the ignorant ones. Hosea 4:6: *"My people are destroyed for lack of knowledge..."*

4. ALTARS AS INSTRUMENTS OF CONTROL AND INTIMIDATION

The Scripture clearly states that no enchantment or divination fashioned against us shall prosper *(Numbers 23:23)*. One of the easiest ways in which the evil ones control and intimidate their victims is through divination or sorcery activities.

There are people who experience emotional fluctuations, from one mood swing to another, without obvious reasons. Their states of mind are usually cluttered with all sorts of negative thoughts and imaginations. Their nightmares and satanic encounters are abnormal, and most times quite frightening.

Some people hardly sleep, for once they close their physical eyes all sorts of horrible and fearful situations begin to unfold themselves. They can see demon-like objects always around them. These sorts of people live in spiritual bondage and imprisonment. Their lives have been shattered by the demonic images that torment and intimidate them.

I have counselled people who told me of their encounters with demonic beings. Others perceive snakes and evil creatures to be always around them. Frequently the cause is satanic or occultic. These people are suffering from generational foundations that were sold out to demonic strongholds. In some cases, people suppressed by such demonic connections strive with much effort but invariably achieve little. Their achievements are never commensurate with the quality of time, effort, money or attention given to the assignment in question.

Deliverance for such people is naturally difficult and stressful. Even when they are born-again, they must make more spiritual efforts to witness some tangible results. People with such foundations must live a life of fasting and prayer if they ever wish to be in control of their destinies and spiritual development.

As instruments of intimidation, altars can be used to deny people their independence.

There are those who cannot function independently, suffering from 'dependence syndrome'. Some wicked parents or mothers or fathers-in-law use such altars to keep their children in check. This is commonly noticeable among wealthy families. Parents in such families use the fear of the riches 'flying away' to erect altars so their children are in perpetual fear that they cannot take any decision without parental approval or consent. The spiritual implication of such satanic control is that the altar becomes a snare unto them, even when the parents are no longer alive.

The only way out for such people is to submit their lives to Jesus Christ, who will become the author and finisher of their faith *(Hebrews 12:2)*. The Holy Spirit dwelling within them casts out that spirit of fear implanted by their parents. God is not the author of fear, but the devil uses fear as an instrument of intimidation *(2 Timothy 1:7)*. As children of God, He has delivered us from the power, authority and stronghold of fear in our lives.

Altars in the hand of the wicked ones may be utilised as instruments of affliction, fear, control, intimidation, and even as weapons of warfare. The particular effectiveness of demonic altars in harming people's well-being is that most persons under altar attack do not know they are being attacked. This is because these altars are erected secretly. For example, the children of Israel did not know that Balak hired Balaam to curse the blessings of God upon their lives *(Numbers 23)*. However, as God had a covenant relationship with the Israelites, Balaam could not curse them.

However, there are some manifestations or signs of attacks from demonic or satanic altars.

CHAPTER 4

MANIFESTATIONS OR SYMPTOMS OF ATTACKS FROM EVIL ALTARS

Based on our counselling experiences, as well as insights from some deliverance ministers and a former occultist who eventually became a Minister of God, the underlisted symptoms may not be exhaustive, but are likely manifestations of attacks orchestrated or executed from evil altars.

However, it is important to note that some of the negative manifestations listed in this chapter may not necessarily be indicative of attacks from evil altars. They may well be as a result of our actions or reactions, either in physical or spiritual matters. As we all know, we are reapers of the fruit of our actions and reactions. The Scripture clearly states:

"Be not deceived; God is not mocked: for whatsoever a man soweth, that shall he also reap." (Galatians 6:7).

Be that as it may, negative manifestations of attacks from evil altars may take the following forms:

1. CONSTANT OR PERIODIC AFFLICTIONS, SICKNESS OR DISEASE

Generally, when affliction, sickness or disease takes the same pattern among family members, this could be the result of attack from an evil altar. Once an altar is raised against a family for affliction or attack, the demons who have been sent on assignment against such families afflict their victims with the same nature of sickness.

For example, if the arrow of stroke has been sent from an evil altar erected against a family, the victims of that attack suffer from the same manner of stroke. They are unlikely to suffer from a liver or kidney problem or any other ailment, but always the same stroke affliction.

The case of Ama's family (not his real name) is quite pathetic. They lost four promising and well-educated men within the space of twenty months. They came under sudden stroke attack, one after the other, beginning with the first son, to the fourth son. The stroke afflictions did not come upon them all from day one. Instead, after the burial of each one, the next person in line became afflicted with the sickness. It was when we were praying for the fourth one that it was disclosed, through revelation, that an altar had been erected against them in their father's compound using their family's pictures and other personal items for evil manipulation and destruction. Although the fourth young man, who was brought from the USA, eventually died, his other siblings never came under such attack after prophetic prayers and intervention destroyed the evil altar.

If cancer has been projected against a family from an evil altar, most members of that family will come under the same cancerous afflictions. They are unlikely to suffer from any other sickness.

The case of Ode's family (not his real name) reveals how a particular disease would have ravaged the whole family, were it not for the intervention of God. This intervention came as a result of the confession of their uncle, who admitted his evil deeds at the point of death.

The story is this: Ode's family suffered from an unknown blood disease which was later discovered to be cancerous. The disease was only evident when it had become terminal. Ode's family are well educated. There are medical doctors and other medical professionals among them, so they were not ignorant of the need to have regular medical check-ups, and this was not a big deal cost-wise. In fact, two of them owned one of the best diagnostic health centres in a European country.

Some time ago, it was discovered that their most senior family member had this terminal blood condition. After his death, the second and third ones had the same problem and died the same way.

A distant relation had the revelation that one of their uncles was behind this, as a result of envy. He had contracted an evil man who had erected an altar of affliction against this family. Before he died, he confessed his wicked deeds and the evil altar was uprooted spiritually. That ended the attacks on the family, but only after much pain had been caused to both the immediate and extended family members.

As with afflictions, so it is in blessings.

Families or individuals who have been attacked from an evil altar concerning their livelihood find that the siblings from that family all begin to experience business failures in one form or manner. Eventually, they will all suffer the same frustrations or failures, either in their businesses or employment, or in other financial or commercial endeavours.

Mr Okafor (not his real name) and his siblings were doing very well in their trade, which they effectively dominated. They were the toast of the banks because of their business connections. I was working as an Area Manager of a leading bank in Nigeria then, and the bank had quite a lucrative business relationship with them.

One day when I visited them, the Chairman of the company told me how they had seen some sacrifices within the business premises. From our discussions, I could discern that he did not consider it a serious issue. When I advised him to seek the advice of his pastor, pointing out that this matter was spiritual, he laughed and said that over the years they had been doing such things without any effect.

Less than six months after this incident, the company began to experience a downturn in business. First, they had problems with their suppliers overseas, with whom they had been dealing for the past fifteen years. The goods imported from this company were substandard and Customs and Excise seized the containers.

Secondly, they invested well over 500,000,000 (five hundred million Nigerian Naira) in a perishable item and, for no reason, the goods were impounded at the seaport for eight months. After investigations, it was discovered that the government had impounded the wrong ship, acting on false information.
Thirdly, they made a bad investment that

wrecked them. In less than two years, a previously booming company became bankrupt. Two of the directors among the family members lost their lives, and an acrimonious legal tussle ensued among the siblings. One of the siblings, who was a bit knowledgeable spiritually, invited some men of God to look into the matter, and the company's downfall was traced to the activities of evil altars initiated by their business competitors.

We have equally counselled people where all the girls in the family, despite being well educated with good moral and Christian backgrounds, remained unmarried. Such a situation could be a result of envy from close relations, which may be a classic case of household enemies erecting evil altars.

Cases of families not having male children could also be a result of evil altar attack. According to a former native doctor whom

God touched, such evil altars concerning male children are erected using plantain leaves, the stem of plantain or unripe plantain, a male effigy of the victim, a piece of the victim's cloth, and other materials. Thereafter, enchantments with some evil incantations are made, to project that their victim will never have a male child.

There are one or two lessons we can learn about the actions of satanic altars:

a) Most wicked altars are initiated by household enemies, and in most cases they are a result of envy. That is why the Scripture says that a man's foes are members of his household *(Matthew 10:38)*. The success or failure of siblings or other family members is an activator or facilitator of such acts – more so in a polygamous family setting.

b) Altars erected by household enemies are usually very effective compared to altars erected by outsiders or unrelated persons. This is because household enemies have the advantages of proximity to, insight into, and knowledge of, their victims, which may not be available to outsiders.

2. SOCIO-EMOTIONAL ISSUES

The following symptoms may be the result of demonic altar attack or manipulation:
• Alienation
• Rejection
• Loneliness
• Perversion
• Depression
• Bitterness
• Low self-esteem
• Feelings of being condemned

The story of Sister Rose (not her real name) exemplifies some of these issues. Sister Rose was married to an ambassador when she discovered her husband was having an affair with his secretary in the office. From then on she became alienated and withdrawn, and slipped into serious depression.

In her dreams she kept seeing herself in a strange altar, where she was fighting a lady whom she did not initially know. She later discovered that the lady was a friend of her husband and had an unhealthy relationship with him, leading to her having a child by him.

From this story, one can easily see the role played by evil altars in this matter. What the lady was doing was practising divination and sorcery with the name of Sister Rose in order to afflict her and bind her spirit. This resulted in her being alienated from her husband, eventually affecting her marriage as she later moved out of her husband's house.

Another good example is the case of Mrs Obor (not her real name). This lady suddenly developed feelings of hatred and low self-esteem, and decided to move out of her matrimonial home after twelve years of marriage. All attempts by her husband and his close relations to settle the matter amicably and make her come back failed. Two months later, the husband remarried to a much younger lady.

After this remarriage, Mrs Obor seemed to return to her senses almost immediately, later beginning to make attempts to come back to her marriage, albeit when it was already too late. She kept saying that she never knew what had happened to her, or why she had decided to leave her husband and four children for a man who was, financially, very well-to-do.

The issue in this matter is that an evil altar was used to pray Mrs Obor out of her matrimonial home. Furthermore, in my own judgment, the husband was also a party to this act because the way he remarried, only after two months, was quite suspicious.

3. PSYCHO-EMOTIONAL ISSUES

Most people who have unusual, persistent fears, undue anxiety and suffer sleepless nights may be suffering from foundational relationships with evil altars. They may exhibit:

- Insomnia
- Various phobias (fears)
- Bipolar disorder
- Unclean thoughts and fantasies
- Living in denial

Based on my counselling experiences, I have met numerous persons whose parents are into demonic activities, have connections with demonic altars, and are committed idol worshippers. Most often, these people are afflicted with such psycho-emotional symptoms due to them being lodged in the house of Satan through their parents' activities. Satan is the sole author of fear.

Such people are usually in the bondage of such spirits, causing them to exhibit the aforementioned symptoms.

For example, Dr Jones (not her real name) was a medical doctor married to a professional, with five children together. However, despite their seemingly comfortable lifestyle, they had never enjoyed peace in their home. The wife kept suspecting the husband of cheating, so she herself lived an adulterous life in order to get back at him. Of course they kept having quarrels, so they both came to me for counselling.

In the course of one of our discussions, the lady opened up to me privately and began to tell me of how her father used to take her to different altars and shrines for initiations. Again, her situation was a case of evil altars. Because her father had more than eight wives, this affected all the daughters in the family such that those who were married were always suspicious and lived double lives. The only way to deal with such issues is to be a committed and uncompromising Christian.

4. FRIGHTENING/TERRIBLE NIGHTMARES

A lot of people experience terrors in the night. Many of them may be under demonic attacks from evil altars, which make them fearful of the night because of extreme nightmare experiences that can affect them emotionally. Such persons may be manipulated spiritually, and demonic forces released against them. This accounts for unexplainable dreams in which they encounter frightening figures and objects, fearful valleys, evil forests, and falling down from terrifying heights.

If these nightmares continue over time, the demons will affect the person's mind-set, and weird behaviours or mannerisms, or even thoughts of suicide, can take a stronghold. Such people may act out their thoughts.

Most cases of inexplicable deaths or suicides of celebrities may be a result of attacks projected by colleagues using evil altars. Those who go into satanic covenants in order to achieve fame, in the end also suffer from such nightmares – which explains why some of them die the way that they do. For example, cases of celebrities who must 'deaden' themselves before they can sleep because of terrible and unbearable experiences at night are a clear manifestation of spiritual terrorism. As a way of 'escape', they prefer to blackout such experiences in their state of rest or dreaming.

5. ABNORMAL SOUNDS OR NOISES

Abnormal sounds or noises may be an indicator of an evil altar in operation. There are times in some homes, offices or places of worship when strange noises, voices or footsteps are distinctly heard. Over time, such noises or sounds may become regulated at particular times of the day or night. This is a clear indication that an evil altar is in operation.

Some people hear their names being called out without seeing any person. The case of Mrs Abiam (not her real name) is very instructive. Mrs Abiam is a pastor's wife, and was expecting home her husband, who had been taking part in a programme. She was in her kitchen cooking, and at the time her husband was supposed to arrive she heard a knock at the door. When she opened the door, there was nobody there. She became expectantly anxious about her husband's arrival. Barely thirty minutes later, the knock at the door repeated, and still nobody was at the door. This happened up to four times, and then suddenly she ran out of the house and became unconscious of her environment.

She was taken to the hospital, but the medics could not work out what was wrong with her. Apparently, she appeared to be normal but became withdrawn and fearful of her environment. The pastor (her husband) later brought his wife to the church and we did some deliverance prayers for her. Thereafter, she regained self-consciousness and became normal on the third day.

This is a clear case of an evil altar in operation. What the evil ones were doing was calling her name through invocation from an evil altar, and when she responded to the knock she had an encounter with the evil spirit. In such cases we advise that, when you answer a strange knock or voice without any visible person calling, your first reaction should be to bind the voice invoking or calling your name for evil, using the name of our Lord Jesus Christ. Repetitions of such prayers over time, or from time to time, may be quite helpful in silencing demonic or satanic invocations through evil altars.

There are cases we have handled involving hearing voices or footsteps walking about in people's homes. Such homes are under satanic or demonic attack through the use of evil altars. Their occupants are being monitored by strange spirits and, if not checked, may over time become vulnerable to strange afflictions, nightmare experiences, diseases, and setbacks in their businesses and marital relationships.

Dr Oni's case (not his real name) is quite telling. Dr Oni moved into the new place he had built for himself and was doing well as a medical doctor. Over time, he noticed the strange sound of steps walking up and down above the ceiling of his house. When the noise persisted, he decided to fumigate the whole house, but the regularity of the noise increased. One thing strange about the noise was that it only occurred in the middle of the night, between 11.30pm and 1.00am.

Dr Oni's wife decided to bring the matter to our attention. We knew straightaway that it was the activity of evil spirits occasioned from evil altars. A night vigil was held during the hours of the strange movement, and the noise ceased, as per Dr Oni's subsequent testimony.

If one is faced with such a situation, the first thing to do is pray around the property prophetically with men or women of God who are anointed. There are some instances where people have ignored such abnormal noises in their homes, and some have ended up facing divorce or a broken marriage, or have been afflicted with strange diseases, because they chose to remain in ignorance.

Closely related to Dr Oni's story is the story of the Osaifo family (not their real name). This incident affected the twins in the household, who were less than fourteen months old. The problem was that between the hours of 12.30 and 1.00 o'clock in the night, the twins would wake up as a peculiar noise began to move around in the ceiling of their house. The children would become restless and be crying. As long as the noise continued, they would continue crying. If the noise lasted for ten minutes, they would be awake for ten minutes, and if it lasted for thirty minutes, they would be awake and crying for the same period.

At first, the parents decided to move the children to a different room. This did not have any effect on the abnormal noise and the reaction of the children. In order to put an end to the situation, some men of God were invited for house cleansing.

During the prayer intercession, the new housemaid confessed that, feeling she was being mistreated by the mother of the twins, she had taken pictures of the babies and sent them to an 'uncle' from her own town, who apparently was a native doctor. He used the pictures to raise an evil altar against the children, as a retaliation to the perceived injustice being meted to her by the twins' mother. The strange noise, and the reaction of the children, stopped as soon as the matter was resolved amicably and the housemaid sent away.

6. EVIL MARKS

The death of my brother opened my eyes to the effectiveness of evil marks being placed on people. Evil marks on our bodies, properties, homes, and so on, are a strong indication that somebody, or someone's property, is under attack from an evil altar.

Marks that you see on people or property are from a particular altar and for a particular purpose, because marks are a form of identification in the spiritual and physical realms. For example, demonic marks for accident are different from marks meant for affliction or disease; marks for disease are different from those meant for frustration;

and marks for frustration are different from near-success syndrome marks. Such marks are equally different from marks meant for disfavour, shame or scandal, which are different again from marks meant for the arrow. That is why the Scripture says that they placed a mark for the arrow upon Jeremiah *(Lamentation 3:12)*. No wonder Apostle Paul said:

> *"From henceforth let no man trouble me: for I bear in my body the marks of the Lord Jesus."* *(Galatians 6:17)*.

By implication, Paul knew he had a mark that was not of God, and when he encountered Jesus he realised that he had been marked for greatness, signs and wonders.

There are numerous persons ignorantly carrying different marks. Some are given these marks willingly by satanic or demonic agents as a signpost of occultic comradeship. They bear a mark on purpose for selfish reasons.

However, most people who have been marked for destruction, frustration, barrenness, fruitlessness, accident, afflictions, scandal or disgrace, and numerous other negative things, have been done so by the wicked ones using their satanic altar base. Regrettably, they are ignorant, and therefore are subjected to all kinds of demonic attacks, manipulations, manifestations, and even destruction.

For example, my late brother had six lacerations on his body with a strange sign. Straight away, I knew this was an evil mark, and did not support his undergoing the operation that eventually killed him. He refused completely. He did not understand that the marks were placed to bring about the afflictions from which he was suffering, and that these afflictions came after he saw the marks on his body. Every effort was made by the family to convince him that the matter was spiritual and not physical, yet he refused.

This was a clear case of a mark of death, and of evil-doers manipulating him from their satanic coven and altar. According to the Scriptures, such people's minds have been darkened *(Ephesians 4:18)*, and because my brother was in a position to take any decision he wanted, nobody could stop him.

For the Nwabu family (not their real name), all the male children – about five well educated young men – died in motor accidents within a space of four to five years. Such accident proneness is a result of satanic marks. The family had been earmarked for accident.

It is vital to note, however, that not every mark one sees on one's body or property is an evil or demonic mark; it could just be a mark inadvertently placed by somebody, or by one's self, knowingly or unknowingly. Nowadays, it is fashionable to have all kinds of tattoos on one's body. For many, it is what they like or want to do in order to belong, and they may not associate any meaning to such drawings on their bodies.

However, that does not remove the spiritual implications of having certain kinds of drawings on one's body. Symbols and drawings have spiritual meaning, and they have the capacity to attract demonic influences upon the person involved. Consider, for example, those who have tattoos of pythons, skulls, or other demonically inclined symbols. Such things can open doors to demonic attacks and manipulations in their lives, which may negatively affect them. Some may be ignorant of the spiritual consequences of such acts, but that does not exempt them from the resulting negative effects.

Just as in the realm of man, where ignorance of any country's law is never an excuse for people whose actions are against that law, spiritually as well, the Scripture says that some perish for lack of knowledge *(Hosea 4:6)*. Ignorance in spiritual matters has destroyed many who have ignored strange markings on their bodies or properties.

The Scripture clearly warns that we should not have tattoos on our bodies:

> *"Ye shall not make any cuttings in your flesh for the dead, nor print any marks upon you: I am the Lord."*
> *(Leviticus 19:28).*

Demonic or satanic marks are therefore points of contact that the wicked ones use against their victims. That is why, as children of God, we ought solely to have on our bodies the marks of our Lord Jesus Christ, as Apostle Paul admonished in Galatians 6:17. In the realm of the spirit, every altar has a mark that defines its purpose.

In the next chapter, there are some prayer points that are Biblically derived, which can be used to deal with powers, authorities and thrones that control evil altars. For anyone to actualise what God has ordained for them, they must be in a position to overthrow and destroy altars that may be erected either to hinder them or to fight what God has ordained for them. According to the Scripture:

"...The effectual fervent prayer of a righteous man availeth much."
(James 5:16).

It is no wonder that God commanded Moses to overthrow and destroy the altars of the inhabitants of the land *(Exodus 34:13)*. When Prophet Elijah wanted to move forward and turn the hearts of the people back to God, he destroyed the evil altars of his time *(1 Kings 18)*. Gideon, as well, embarked on overthrowing altars of darkness in order to actualise what God had ordained for his people *(Judges 6:24-28)*. David, being established as the king of Israel, burned the images of his enemies, the Philistines *(2 Samuel 5:17)*. These are just a few examples of the numerous kings and men of God who destroyed the evil altars of their times.

In the new dispensation, apart from being sealed with the marks of Jesus Christ, we need to deal with the evil altars and strongholds in our lives, spiritually and physically, using the name and the blood of Jesus. This is the prophetic aspect of our faith – applying the Word of God prophetically to achieve a purpose, through prayer *(James 2:17)*.

CHAPTER 5

PRAYER POINTS

1. **PSALM 11:3** – O Lord my God, my Redeemer and Saviour, because Jesus Christ is my Lord and Saviour, I use the name and the blood of Jesus Christ to separate myself and my family members from satanic, demonic, occultic, marine and witchcraft altars that are active or operating in our father's, mother's, wife's or husband's foundation, in Jesus' name, Amen.

b. O Lord my God, my Redeemer and Saviour, I release the fire of God upon every foundational, ancestral and family altar where the umbilical cords, hairs, body parts and/or garments of myself and my family members have been kept for evil purposes, in Jesus' name, Amen.

2. **1 SAMUEL 28:13** – O Lord my God, my Redeemer and Saviour, I use the name and blood of Jesus Christ to bind and paralyse evil and demonic spirits that dwell on the earth and that are assigned to hinder me and my family members, in Jesus' name, Amen.

3. **EPHESIANS 6:12** – O Lord my God, my Redeemer and Saviour, I use the name and blood of Jesus Christ to destroy and nullify demonic or satanic agreements between rulers of darkness in high places and occultic or demonic forces of the earth fashioned against me and my family members, in Jesus' name, Amen.

4. **REVELATION 17:1** – O Lord my God, my Redeemer and Saviour, I use the name and blood of Jesus Christ to destroy and nullify evil agreements between marine spirits and demonic forces of the earth, fashioned against me and my family members, in Jesus' name, Amen.

5. **EXODUS 20:4** – O Lord my God, my Redeemer and Saviour, I use the name of Jesus Christ to command Holy Ghost fire to consume altars of the earth where graven images are being used to project negative energy or aura against me and my family members, in Jesus' name, Amen.

6. **EZEKIEL 21:21** – O Lord my God, my Redeemer and Saviour, any strongman or woman that will ever raise altars at T junctions, roundabouts or crossroads to use divination, enchantment or invocation in order to release arrows of affliction, sickness, accident or death against me and my family members, will forever fail, in Jesus' name, Amen.

7. **EXODUS 20:24** – O Lord my God, my Redeemer and Saviour, I decree and declare that demonic, occultic or satanic altars of the earth that will ever harbour the names, pictures, body parts, garments, etc., of

myself and my family members as a point of contact to fight or afflict us, will receive the fire of God, in Jesus' name, Amen.

8. **EXODUS 20:25** – O Lord my God, my Redeemer and Saviour, my Rock of Ages, I use the blood of Jesus Christ to cancel and nullify the effects of any altar of stone energised with satanic oil or blood, being used to fight me and my family members, in Jesus' name, Amen.

9. **ISAIAH 40:22** – O Lord my God, my Redeemer and Saviour, I use the name of Jesus Christ to command the Angels of God to destroy satanic or demonic circles of altars of the earth, where the names of myself and my family members are being mentioned for shame, evil, stagnancy or limitation, in Jesus' name, Amen.

10. **MATTHEW 16:18** – O Lord my God, my Redeemer and Saviour, I decree and declare

that demonic or satanic gates of the earth erected to hinder me and my family members have been destroyed by the Angels of God, in Jesus' name, Amen.

11. **HOSEA 13:14** – O Lord my God, my Redeemer and Saviour, I decree and declare that altars of the earth in any graveyard, being used to project evil outcomes against me and my family members, have been destroyed by the Angels of God, in Jesus' name, Amen.

12. **NUMBERS 23:1** – O Lord my God, my Redeemer and Saviour, I command the Angels of God to destroy altars of the earth where blood sacrifices of four-legged animals, marine creatures, fowls of the air, creeping things, animals that live on trees and human-beings are being used against me and my family members, in Jesus' name, Amen.

13. **JEREMIAH 22:29** – O Lord my God, my Redeemer and Saviour, I decree and declare that anyone who will ever use the earth as an instrument to curse me and my family members will never succeed, in Jesus' name, Amen.

14. **1 CHRONICLES 21:29** – O Lord my God, my Redeemer and Saviour, I decree and declare that any satanic or demonic altars of the earth that will ever be erected against me and my family members, will forever fail, in Jesus' name, Amen.

15. **ISAIAH 56:9** – O Lord my God, my Redeemer and Saviour, I decree and declare that satanic or demonic altars that will ever be erected in any evil forest in order to destroy God's purpose for me and my family members' lives, will forever be consumed by Holy Ghost fire, in Jesus' name, Amen.

16. **EZEKIEL 6:13A** – O Lord my God, my Redeemer and Saviour, I decree and declare that any satanic, demonic or evil altar that will ever be erected upon any hill or hills, meant to hinder me and my family members, will fail forever, in Jesus' name, Amen.

17. **EZEKIEL 8:16** – O Lord my God, my Redeemer and Saviour, I decree and declare that demonic or satanic temples of the earth that will ever be used to fight the well-being of myself and my family members will forever be consumed by Holy Ghost fire, in Jesus' name, Amen.

18. **2 KINGS 17:11** – O Lord my God, my Redeemer and Saviour, I decree and declare that demonic or satanic altars of incense meant to hinder my destiny and that of my family members shall fail forever, and I command the east wind to carry the evil incense back to its senders, in Jesus' name, Amen.

19. **MATTHEW 10:36** – O Lord my God, my Redeemer and Saviour, I decree and declare that demonic or satanic altars of darkness, erected by household enemies against me and my family members, will forever fail, in Jesus' name, Amen.

20. **ISAIAH 54:15** – O Lord my God, my Redeemer and Saviour, I decree and declare that whenever evil men or women gather against me and my family members, in their covens or upon their evil altars, the Angels of God will forever scatter them, in Jesus' name, Amen.

21. **REVELATION 16:7** – O Lord my God, my Redeemer and Saviour, I use the name and blood of Jesus Christ to silence any voice or voices from evil altars that will ever cry or speak against me and my family members, in Jesus' name, Amen.

22. **PSALM 121:6-7** – O Lord my God, my Redeemer and Saviour, I decree and declare that demonic or satanic altars in the body of the heavenlies (the sun, moon and stars) will never be used to fight me and my family members, in Jesus' name, Amen.

23. **ACTS 17:17** – O Lord my God, my Redeemer and Saviour, I decree and declare that satanic, demonic or occultic altars erected in a marketplace against me and my family members will forever fail, in Jesus Name, Amen.

b. O Lord my God, my Redeemer and Saviour, I decree and declare that satanic, demonic or occultic altars that will ever harbour the names, body parts, items of clothing or personal effects of myself and my family members will be consumed by Holy Ghost fire, in Jesus' name, Amen.

24. **JEREMIAH 33:25** – O Lord my God, my Redeemer and Saviour, I decree and declare that the ordinances of the heaven, earth and water realms that control altars will never hinder the well-being of myself and my family members, in Jesus' name, Amen.

25. **EZEKIEL 35:6** – O Lord my God, my Redeemer and Saviour, I use the blood of Jesus Christ to cancel and nullify any demonic, satanic or occultic blood crying against the well-being of myself and my family members, in Jesus' name, Amen.

26. **EXODUS 34:13** – O Lord my God, my Redeemer and Saviour, I command the Holy Ghost Fire to destroy any demonic, satanic or occultic altar of darkness fashioned against the blessing of myself and my family members, in Jesus' name, Amen.

27. **NUMBERS 23:1** – O Lord my God, my Redeemer and Saviour, I command the

Angels of God to overthrow and destroy demonic, satanic or occultic altars of seven that have been erected against the blessing of myself and my family members, in Jesus' name, Amen.

28. **2 KINGS 21:5** – O Lord my God, my Redeemer and Saviour, I decree and declare that demonic, satanic or evil altars erected to the host of heaven, meant to hinder the well-being of myself and my family members, are destroyed by the Angels of God, in Jesus' name, Amen.

29. **2 CHRONICLES 23:17** – O Lord my God, my Redeemer and Saviour, I decree and declare that any demonic, satanic or evil priests that will ever be hired to curse me and my family members before their altars, will never succeed, in Jesus' name, Amen.

30. **1 KINGS 13:2** – O Lord my God, my Redeemer and Saviour, I will forever bless

Your name because voices in demonic or satanic altars of darkness will never understand my future or destiny, or those of my family members, in Jesus' name, Amen.

31. **HEBREWS 7:26-27** – O Lord my God, my Redeemer and Saviour, I will forever bless Your name because Jesus Christ is the High Priest of myself and my family members, and the Cross of Jesus Christ as a powerful altar will forever speak in our favour, in Jesus' name, Amen.

CHAPTER 6

HOW TO RAISE AN ALTAR

1. EMPTY PLOT OF LAND

In Genesis 28:18-22, we see the story of Jacob who had an encounter with God as he lay his head on a stone. He later used that stone to build an altar unto God. Therefore, in building an altar on an empty plot of land, the first thing to use is stone. Stones are permanent and immovable, and they will remain in the position in which they are placed. The number of stones required is twelve. Why? In Joshua 4:5,20, Joshua commanded the men from each tribe to pick up a stone, which he later used to erect an altar; the number of stones was twelve. Following this example, place three stones at each of the four corners of the plot of land. The next step is to pour anointing oil upon the stones, since Jacob poured oil upon the stone that he used as an altar, as we see in Genesis 28:18. The anointing oil signifies the presence of God. Therefore, the oil on the stone is an indication of the continual abiding presence of God upon that altar of stone. In Genesis 32:25-32, Jacob returned to the place where he first encountered God, and he still encountered God there after many years.

The next step is to use salt. The salt brings the land into covenant with God and establishes that land as your own from God forever. The Bible illustrates this:

> *"Ought ye not to know that the Lord God of Israel gave the kingdom over Israel to David for ever, even to him and to his sons by a covenant of salt?"*
> *(2 Chronicles 13:5).*

Pour the salt upon the stones and oil, then use the same oil and salt to connect the three-stone altars at each of the four corners of the property to chain the whole land.

2. FOUNDATION OF BUILDING

Before building a house or structure on a plot of land, we also need to build an altar in the foundation. This altar transforms the whole building into an altar. When the foundation is being dug, stones also need to be used to build this altar. In Matthew 16:18, Jesus said: *"And I say also unto thee, That thou art Peter, and upon this rock I will build my church; and the gates of hell shall not prevail against it."* Jesus was referring to the foundation of the Church that he would build, and used a rock, which of course is a large stone, to denote this fact.

Also, Isaiah 28:16 refers to the foundational stone, which is "a sure foundation". Therefore, to lay an altar in the foundation of a house, one uses a big stone or a heap of stones, using anointing oil and salt just as in raising altars for an empty plot of land. The blood of Jesus is also applied to the stone as a witness to continually speak on that foundational altar – Hebrews 12:24 and 1 John 5:8 exemplify this.

3. DEDICATED ROOM OF A HOUSE

When your building is completed, you need to dedicate a room as an altar of God in your house – the Bible shows examples of this in 1 Kings 17:17-24 and 2 Kings 4:8-34. Even evil men have a room dedicated to their demons, though nobody enters that room. However, in the case of a child of God, the dedicated room is for the whole family. Even though Abraham was always on the move, he built an altar unto God everywhere he pitched his tent, as recorded in Genesis 12:7-8 and Genesis 13:18.

4. RENTED BUILDING

In a rented building you can still raise an altar of stones unto God. If there is a garden, you should use stones, oil and salt as previously described. Inside the building, you should use oil, earth, blood and stones to raise altars in each of the rooms in your rented accommodation. You should also consistently play Christian music in your rented home to spiritualise it. Such a practice was implemented by David in 1 Samuel 16:23 to drive away the evil spirit from Saul.

5. OFFICE/PLACE OF WORK

If you share an office, you can turn the chair that you use into an altar by anointing it with oil and the blood of Jesus, and dedicate it to the Lord Jesus Christ. In your free time, pray as you sit on the chair to continually spiritualise it. If you have an office to yourself, use stones, oil, blood and salt at the four corners as described in raising an altar in an empty plot of land. Again, spiritualise your office with prayer and anointed songs of praise and worship.